HAL•LEONARD
INSTRUMENTAL
PLAY-ALONG

VIOLIN

STEPHEN SONDHEIM BROADWAY SOLOS

CONTENTS

THE CD IS PLAYABLE ON ANY CD PLAYER, AND IS ALSO ENHANCED SO MAC AND PC USERS CAN ADJUST THE RECORDING TO ANY TEMPO WITHOUT CHANGING THE PITCH.

ISBN 978-1-4234-7283-4

RILTING MUSIC, INC.

EXCLUSIVELY DISTRIBUTED BY

HAL•LEONARD®
CORPORATION
7777 W. BLUEMOUND RD. P.O. BOX 13819 MILWAUKEE, WI 53213

Visit Hal Leonard Online at
www.halleonard.com

ANYONE CAN WHISTLE

from ANYONE CAN WHISTLE

1/2

VIOLIN

Words and Music by
STEPHEN SONDHEIM

Moderately

Strings

Play

mp

mf *a tempo*

rit.

f

Broadly

rit.

rall.

BEING ALIVE
from COMPANY

Music and Lyrics by
STEPHEN SONDHEIM

3/4
VIOLIN

Moderately

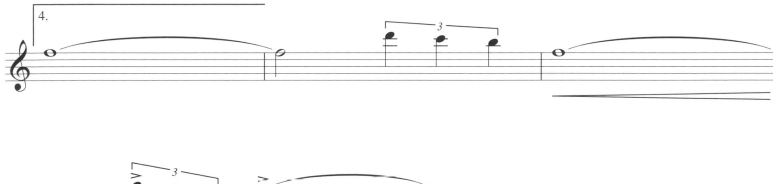

BROADWAY BABY

from FOLLIES

Music and Lyrics by
STEPHEN SONDHEIM

VIOLIN

CHILDREN WILL LISTEN

from INTO THE WOODS

VIOLIN

Words and Music by
STEPHEN SONDHEIM

COMEDY TONIGHT

from A FUNNY THING HAPPENED ON THE WAY TO THE FORUM

Words and Music by
STEPHEN SONDHEIM

VIOLIN

9/10

GOOD THING GOING

from MERRILY WE ROLL ALONG

VIOLIN

Words and Music by
STEPHEN SONDHEIM

JOHANNA
from SWEENEY TODD

Words and Music by
STEPHEN SONDHEIM

13/14
VIOLIN

LOSING MY MIND

from FOLLIES

Music and Lyrics by
STEPHEN SONDHEIM

VIOLIN

NOT A DAY GOES BY

from MERRILY WE ROLL ALONG

17/18

VIOLIN

Words and Music by
STEPHEN SONDHEIM

Slowly, with feeling

NOT WHILE I'M AROUND

from SWEENEY TODD

19/20

VIOLIN

Words and Music by
STEPHEN SONDHEIM

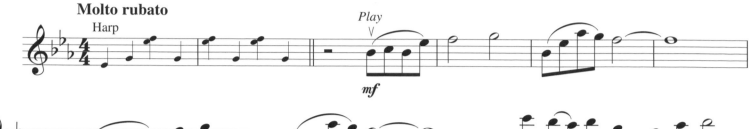

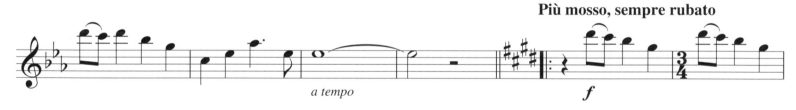

OLD FRIENDS
from MERRILY WE ROLL ALONG

VIOLIN

Words and Music by
STEPHEN SONDHEIM

PRETTY WOMEN

from SWEENEY TODD

VIOLIN

Words and Music by
STEPHEN SONDHEIM

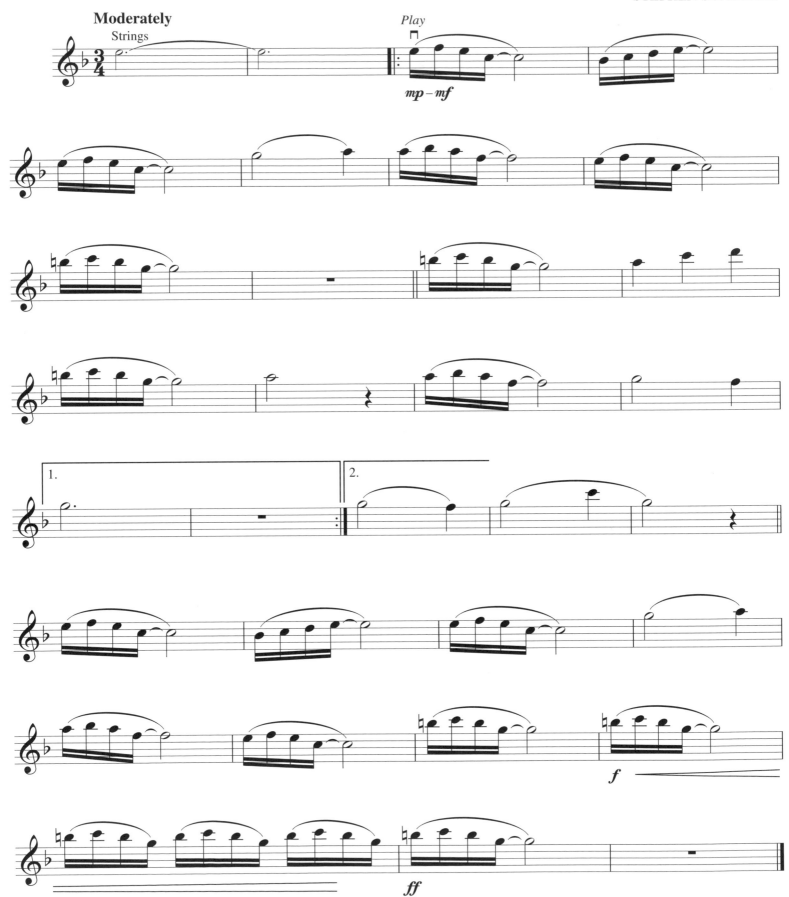

SEND IN THE CLOWNS
from the Musical A LITTLE NIGHT MUSIC

Words and Music by
STEPHEN SONDHEIM

25/26
VIOLIN

SUNDAY
from SUNDAY IN THE PARK WITH GEORGE

Words and Music by
STEPHEN SONDHEIM